Food Chains

Anita Ganeri

Heinemann Library
Chicago, Illinois

Customer Service 888-454-2279
Visit our website at www.heinemannlibrary.com

Editorial: Jilly Attwood, Kate Bellamy
Design: Jo Hinton-Malivoire
Picture research: Ginny Stroud-Lewis, Ruth Blair
Production: Séverine Ribierre

Originated by Dot Gradations Ltd
Printed and bound in China by South China Printing Company

08 07 06 05 04
10 9 8 7 6 5 4 3 2 1

Library of Congress Cataloging-in-Publication Data
Ganeri, Anita, 1961-
   Food chains / Anita Ganeri.
       p. cm. -- (Nature's patterns)
   Includes bibliographical references and index.
   ISBN 1-4034-5878-2 (HC), 1-4034-5884-7 (Pbk.)
   1. Food chains (Ecology)--Juvenile literature. I. Title. II. Series.
   QH541.14.G359 2004
   577'.16--dc22

                              2004000935

Acknowledgments
The author and publishers are grateful to the following for permission to reproduce copyright material:
pp. 4, 19 Corbis; pp. 5, 21 Heather Angel/Natural Visions; p. 6 Gaetano/Corbis; pp. 8 (soil), 9, 20 Getty Images/Photodisc; p. 8 (flower) Tudor Photography; pp. 10, 12, 15, 17, 25, 29 Nature Photo Library; pp. 11, 18 Science Photo Library; p. 13 Roy Waller/NHPA; p. 14 Darek Karp/NHPA; p. 16 NHPA; p. 22 Haroldo Palo Jr./NHPA; p. 23 David Aubrey/Corbis; p. 24 Laurie Campbell/NHPA; pp. 26, 27 Digital Vision

Cover photograph is reproduced with permission of Nature Photo Library.

Our thanks to David Lewin for his assistance in the preparation of this book.

Every effort has been made to contact copyright holders of any material reproduced in this book. Any omissions will be rectified in subsequent printings if notice is given to the publisher.

The paper used to print this book comes from sustainable resources.

Contents

Some words are shown in bold, **like this.** You can find out what they mean by looking in the glossary.

Nature's Patterns

Nature is always changing. Many of the changes in nature follow a **pattern.** This means that they happen over and over again.

Giraffes use their long necks to reach leaves to eat.

This eagle catches a fish with its strong claws.

All animals need to eat to stay alive. Animals are **linked** together in a pattern by the things they eat. All animals need other living things for food.

food chains

Plants and animals are **linked** by the food they need. This **pattern** is called a **food chain.** Each plant or animal is a link in the food chain.

All living things are part of a food chain, including you.

Each link in the food chain is eaten by the next in line. Some food chains are very simple, like the one below.

Plants are eaten by rabbits. In turn, rabbits are eaten by owls.

grasses and seeds → rabbit → owl

Start with Plants

All **food chains** begin with plants. Green plants are the first **link** in the food chain. Plants make their food from sunlight and water.

Sunlight shines down.

Roots take up water.

This butterfly drinks the **nectar** from a flower.

Animals cannot make their own food. They have to move around and find things to eat. Some animals eat plants. Some animals eat other animals.

Plant-Eaters

Some animals eat only plants. After plants, these animals are the next **links** in the **food chain.** They are called **herbivores,** which means plant-eaters.

Caterpillars are herbivores. They eat leaves.

This animal is a **crustacean**. It lives in the sea and eats water plants.

Some herbivores eat leaves or grass.
Some eat fruit, nuts, and seeds.
Others suck **nectar** from flowers.
Some munch on underwater plants.

11

Meat-Eaters

Some animals eat other animals. These animals are the next **link** in the **food chain** after herbivores. They are called **carnivores,** which means meat-eaters.

Birds and their chicks eat caterpillars.

Ringed seals eat **crustaceans**. They crush them with their strong teeth.

Carnivores have special tools for catching their food. Lions and wolves have sharp, pointed teeth. Eagles have sharp, hooked beaks and large claws, called talons.

Eating Plants and Animals

Many animals have a mixed **diet.**
They eat both plants and animals.
These animals are called **omnivores.**

Large birds like this hawk eat smaller birds.

Bears, foxes, raccoons, and people are all omnivores. Raccoons eat fruit, eggs, worms, and bugs. Many people eat fruit, vegetables, meat, and fish.

Polar bears hunt for seals on the ice.

Using Up Waste

In nature, everything is used again. After a plant or animal dies, its body starts to rot. **Fungi,** worms, and **bacteria** eat the dead plant or animal.

Worms, fungi, and bacteria are all called *decomposers*.

Nutrients from dead plants and animals soak into the soil. This makes the soil rich, so plants can grow well. Animals eat these plants and the **food chain** starts all over.

Most fungi live on dead plants and animals.

In the Sea

Food chains happen everywhere. In the sea, there are many different food chains. But they all start with tiny plants in **plankton.**

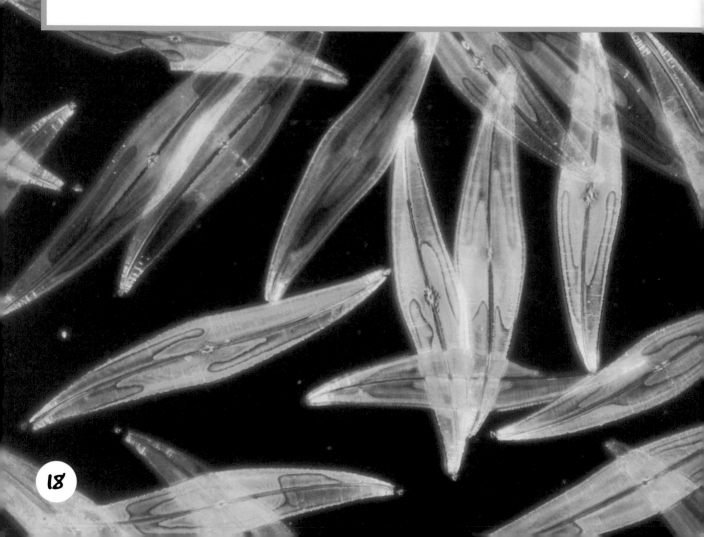

Sharks have sharp teeth for eating meat.

Small animals feed on plankton. Then, these small animals are eaten by fish and larger animals. Then, the fish and larger animals are eaten by even larger animals, such as sharks.

19

Fresh Water

Fresh water is not salty like water in the sea. Fresh water is found in rivers, lakes, and ponds. Each of these places has its own **food chains.**

Water plants are food for snails, fish, and other animals.

In one kind of river food chain, snails eat water plants. Then, fish eat the snails. In turn, large birds called herons catch fish to eat.

In the Rain Forest

It is hot and steamy in a rain forest. Plants grow quickly in the warm, wet weather. Many different animals live among these plants and need them for food.

In a rain forest, there are lots of plants for bugs to eat.

Bugs make tasty snacks for tree frogs.

In one rain forest **food chain,** bugs eat the juicy leaves of trees. Then, tree frogs eat the bugs. The tree frogs are eaten by snakes and birds.

In the woods

Woodland plants and trees are tasty food for animals. The leaves, flowers, bark, fruit, nuts, stems, and roots of these plants can all be eaten.

Squirrels eat nuts, which are full of **nutrients.**

Bats fly around at night to catch moths to eat.

Some woodland animals come out at night to find food. Moths drink flower **nectar.** Bats fly through the darkness to catch juicy moths in midair.

Desert Diets

The dry, dusty desert is not an easy place to live. There is very little to eat and drink. Plants and animals have to look hard to find food.

Camels can go for weeks without drinking. They get some water by eating desert plants.

Desert plants store water. Bugs, such as locusts and crickets, eat the desert plants. Then, lizards and scorpions munch on the juicy bugs.

This desert lizard is looking for bugs to eat.

food Webs

An animal may eat many different things. This animal can be a **link** in different **food chains.** These food chains join up to make a food web.

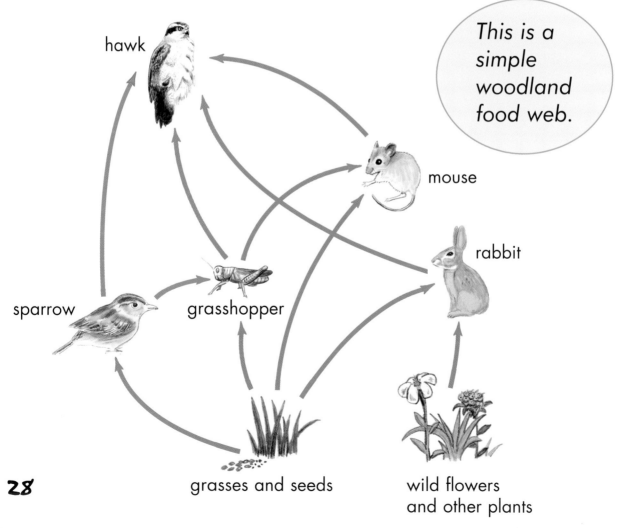

hawk

This is a simple woodland food web.

mouse

rabbit

sparrow

grasshopper

grasses and seeds

wild flowers and other plants

In one food chain in the Arctic, foxes feed on birds that eat fish. The fish eat tiny sea animals. But giant whales also eat these tiny sea animals! All these animals together make a food web.

The Arctic fox catches birds to eat.

Pyramid of Numbers

In a **food chain,** there are more plants than **herbivores.** There are more herbivores than **carnivores** or **omnivores.**

A pyramid can show the number of living things in a food chain. In this pyramid, there is more grass than rabbits and there are more rabbits than owls.

Glossary

bacteria tiny living things

carnivore animal that eats other animals

crustacean animal such as a shrimp or a crab

decomposer living thing that breaks down dead plants and animals

diet what an animal eats

food chain way in which plants and animals are linked by food

fungi (one is called a fungus) living things such as mushrooms

herbivore animal that eats plants

link to join together, or a thing that is connected to something else

nectar sweet liquid inside a flower

nutrient chemical that helps plants and animals grow

omnivore animal that eats plants and animals

pattern something that happens over and over again

plankton very tiny plants and animals that float in the water

More Books to Read

Manning, Mick. *Yum-Yum!* Danbury, Conn.: Scholastic Library, 1998.

Riley, Peter D. *Food Chains.* Danbury, Conn.: Scholastic Library, 1998.

Scott, Janine. *Food Found All Around.* Minneapolis: Compass Point, 2002.

Index